Traditional Stencil Designs from India

Pradumna and Rosalba Tana

Dover Publications, Inc., New York

Published in Canada by General Publishing Company, Ltd., 30 Lesmill Road, Don Mills, Toronto, Ontario.
Published in the United Kingdom by Constable and Company, Ltd.

Traditional Stencil Designs from India is a new work, first published by Dover Publications, Inc., in 1986.

DOVER *Pictorial Archive* SERIES

Manufactured in the United States of America
Dover Publications, Inc., 31 East 2nd Street, Mineola, N.Y. 11501

Library of Congress Cataloging-in-Publication Data

Tana, Pradumna.
  Traditional stencil designs from India.

  (Dover pictorial archive series)
  1. Stencil work—India. 2. Design, Decorative—Plant forms. 3. Design, Decorative—Animal forms. I. Tana, Rosalba. II. Title.
TT270.T36 1986   745.7′3′0222   86-2197
ISBN 0-486-25118-7 (pbk.)

Foreword

The simple yet ingenious designs in this volume are based on the fascinating though little-known traditional Indian art of *sanzi khaka*. This term refers to the paper stencils (*khaka*) used for the floor decorations (*sanzi*) which priests and their assistants execute with marble dust and various powdered colors in the inner sanctuary of several Vaishnav temples (those in which Vishnu and his incarnations, especially Lord Krishna, are worshipped). On major festive occasions, such as Govardhan Puja (Adoration of Mount Govardhan), Basant Panchami (Spring Festival), Holi (Festival of Colors) and Janmashtami (Birthday of Lord Krishna), these temple decorations in the cities of Mathura, Brindaban, Barsana and Nathdwara reveal a wealth of stencil motifs ranging from floral to figurative, from purely decorative to essentially religious.

All the festivals and sites mentioned above are closely associated with the popular divinity Lord Krishna, in whom all nature rejoices. Mathura, Brindaban and Barsana are located on or near the Jumna River (between Delhi and Agra) in Uttar Pradesh state; this was the region in which the incarnate Lord Krishna dwelt as cowherd and prince. Govardhan, in that vicinity, is the mountain that Lord Krishna once held aloft as a gigantic umbrella to shelter his people from a storm. Nathdwara, near the city of Udaipur in Rajasthan, contains an especially sacred Krishna temple. Celebration of the Holi festival includes the playful spraying of one's fellows with colored water; the illustrations on pages 56 and 57 show celebrants carrying syringes for this purpose.

It is heartening to note how, in this era of computers, age-old temple rituals have been instrumental in saving many traditional arts otherwise destined to oblivion. Even today, one can see artisans in the cities of Mathura and Nathdwara busy cutting *sanzi* stencils, which devout pilgrims purchase to carry home as sacred souvenirs. The authors possess several such stencils, which were bought during their study tours of these holy places. The collection presented here includes mostly ornamental motifs and flora and fauna designs.

The authors gratefully acknowledge the wholehearted help extended by Shri Madhavrai Goswami, hereditary priest of the Mota Mandir of Buleshwar-Bombay (as well as an accomplished artist and longtime friend), in permitting them to study and photograph the stencils preserved in the storehouse of his temple. Some of these stencils are decades old, torn and no longer in active use, yet they have provided many of the motifs presented in this book.

4

14

33

34

39

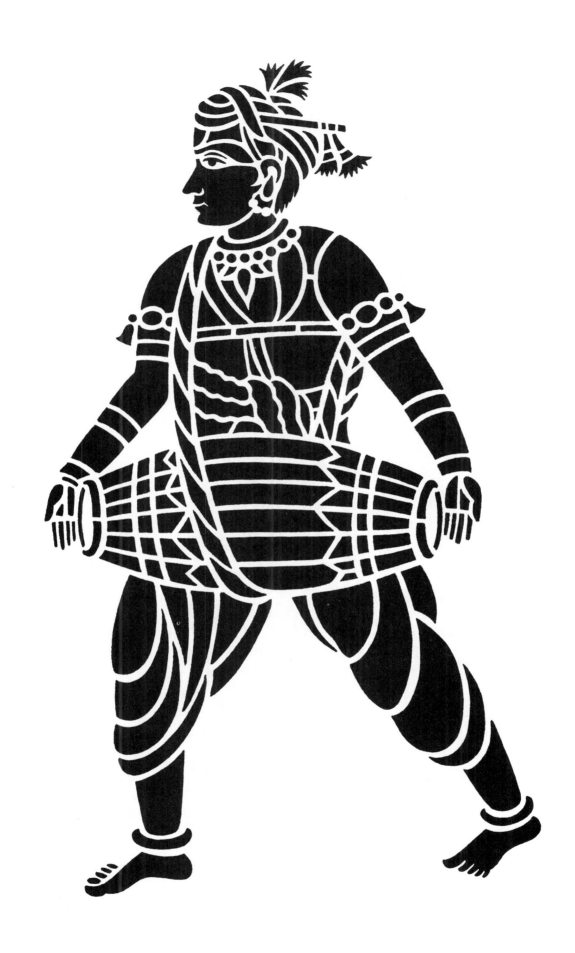

58